Visualization

Acquire Proficiency In The Application Of Visualization
Techniques, Cultivate The Skill Of Self Analysis, And
Foster The Habit Of Engaging In Mindfulness

*(The Pertinence Of Architectural Visualization In The
Realm Of Unconstructed Structures)*

Edgar Victoria

TABLE OF CONTENT

Data Mining Methodologies

Now, let us examine various data mining techniques that can be integrated into the data mining engine. These methodologies enable the identification of concealed, legitimate, and unprecedented patterns and correlations within extensive datasets. These methodologies employ a diverse range of machine learning techniques, mathematical algorithms, and statistical models to address varying inquiries. Some illustrative instances of such algorithms include neural networks, decision trees, classification, and so forth. Data mining primarily utilizes prediction and analysis.

Data mining experts employ various techniques to comprehend, manipulate, and scrutinize data, in order to derive precise conclusions from vast quantities of information. The techniques employed by them rely on diverse technologies and methodologies stemming from the convergence of statistics, machine learning, and database administration. Thus, what strategies do they employ to procure these outcomes?

In the majority of data mining projects, experts have employed various data mining methodologies. Furthermore, they have successfully devised and implemented diverse modules and methodologies encompassing classification, association, prediction, clustering, regression, as well as sequential patterns. We shall delve into a more comprehensive examination of a selection of these topics in the subsequent section of this chapter.

Classification
The classification methodology is utilized to acquire pertinent and

substantial insights into the metadata and data employed in the process of mining. This technique is employed by experts to categorize data points and variables into distinct classifications. A selection of these techniques can be classified as follows:

Data mining frameworks and techniques can be categorized based on the origin of the data being extracted. This procedure is founded upon the information that you utilize or manage. As an illustration, data can be categorized into various types such as time-series data, textual data, multimedia, the World Wide Web, spatial data, and so forth.

Data may be categorized into various frameworks depending on the database employed in the analysis. The classification at hand is predicated upon the particular model being employed. As an illustration, one can categorize the data into the subsequent classifications:

relational database, object-oriented database, transactional database, and so forth.

Data can be categorized within a framework by discerning the type of knowledge derived from the dataset. The aforementioned method of categorization relies on the nature of the information that has been derived from the dataset. In addition, one may utilize the various functionalities employed for the purpose of conducting this classification. Several frameworks employed include clustering, classification, discrimination, characterization, among others.

Data may likewise be categorized within a structured framework, delineated by the various methodologies employed in the process of data mining. This method of categorization is founded on the analytical methodology employed for data extraction, including machine learning, neural networks, visualization, database-focused and data warehouse-focused techniques, genetic algorithms, and so forth. This mode of categorization additionally considers the level of interactivity exhibited by the graphical user interface.

Clustering
Clustering is a computational technique employed to partition data into cohesive sets of interconnected entities, based on their distinctive attributes. When partitioning the dataset into clusters, it is possible to sacrifice certain nuances contained within the dataset, while concurrently enhancing the overall quality of the dataset. When considering the subject of data modeling, it can be observed that clustering finds its foundation in the disciplines of mathematics, numerical analysis, and statistics. In the context of machine

learning, an analysis of the data modeling reveals latent patterns within the dataset, as indicated by the clustering results. The algorithm employed aims to identify groupings within the dataset utilizing unsupervised machine learning techniques. The ensuing framework formulated shall embody a notion of data. When considering the matter from a pragmatic standpoint, this mode of analysis assumes a crucial role in a multitude of data mining applications encompassing text mining, scientific data exploration, spatial database applications, web analysis, customer relationship management, computational biology, information retrieval, medical diagnostics, and the like.

Put simply, clustering analysis represents a data mining approach employed to discern the data points within a dataset that exhibit considerable similarities. This methodology will aid in the identification and differentiation of various similarities and disparities within the dataset. Clustering bears resemblance to classification, wherein sizable segments of data are organized into groups on the basis of their resemblances.

Regression
Regression analysis represents an alternative approach to data mining, utilized for the purpose of examining and determining the association between diverse variables, predicated on the inclusion of another variable within the dataset. This method is employed to determine the likelihood of a particular variable's occurrence within the given dataset. The process of regression encompasses a range of modeling and planning techniques

employed in diverse algorithms. As an illustration, this method can be employed to estimate a cost or expenditure by taking into consideration a range of factors, including consumer demand, competition, and availability. This technique will provide a precise and comprehensive understanding of the interconnection between the variables within the given dataset. Several examples of this methodology include linear regression, multiple regression, logistic regression, among others.

Association Rules

The technique employed by data mining is to establish a correlation between different data points within the dataset. By means of this methodology, experts in data mining possess the capability to discern concealed patterns or trends within the dataset. An association rule constitutes a conditional statement employing the if-then structure, thereby facilitating the discernment of potential correlations among distinct data points within voluminous data sets for the practitioner. Moreover, it is possible to discern associations among diverse databases as well.

The technique of association rule mining finds application in various domains and is frequently employed by retailers to discern patterns and associations within medical and retail data. The algorithm operates in distinct manners when applied to diverse sets of data. As an illustration, you have the option to compile the data of all the items you have acquired within the previous months and apply association rules to discern patterns of items that are frequently purchased together. This analysis will provide insights into items that are commonly grouped together for potential future purchases. Several measurements that are utilized include:

Lift

This metric is utilized to establish the precision of the likelihood of your purchasing a particular product. The calculation employed to achieve this is represented by the formula: (confidence interval) divided by (item A) divided by (the complete data set).

Support

This method is employed to ascertain the frequency at which various items are purchased by an individual, and subsequently compares this information with the aggregate data that has been gathered. The equation utilized for this purpose is as follows: (item C item D) divided by (the complete set of data).

Confidence

This procedure quantifies the frequency with which you acquire a particular item in conjunction with the acquisition of another item. To achieve this objective, it is recommended to utilize the subsequent equation: the division of (item C multiplied by item D) by (item D).

Outer Detection
The outer detection technique is employed in cases where there is a requirement to ascertain the patterns or data points within the dataset that deviate from the anticipated behavior or pattern of the dataset. This methodology frequently finds application in various domains including detection, intrusion prevention, fraud detection, and so forth. Outer detection is alternatively referred to as outlier mining or outlier analysis.
An outlier refers to a data point within the dataset that deviates from the

expected pattern observed in the remaining data points. The majority of data sets typically exhibit the presence of outliers, and this phenomenon should be anticipated. This technique assumes a significant role within the realm of data mining. This method is employed in various domains, including the detection of debit or credit card fraud, identification of outliers in data from wireless sensor networks, and recognition of network interruptions, among others.

Sequential Patterns

A consecutive arrangement is an additional methodology employed in the field of data mining, specifically designed to analyze and assess sequential data patterns within a given dataset. This method is among the most effective approaches for discerning concealed sequential patterns within the dataset. This method employs distinct subsequences derived from a singular sequence, wherein the assessment cannot be quantified based on numerous criteria, such as occurrence frequency, length, and so forth. In more simplified terms, this data mining process enables users to identify and uncover various patterns, whether they are of a small or significant nature, within the transactional data within a specific timeframe.

Prediction
This approach utilizes a fusion of various data mining methodologies and algorithms, including but not limited to clustering, trend analysis, classification, and more. Forecasting utilizes past data, comprising of instances and occurrences, in a sequential manner to anticipate future outcomes.

Ensure Clarity Regarding Your Personal Vision

After determining the specific daily time for meditation and making a firm commitment, the subsequent stage involves establishing clarity regarding your personal vision. It is imperative that you grasp the content of this chapter with utmost clarity, as it holds significant weight in terms of its importance. This is your objective. If your understanding of this concept is unclear, then all of your efforts in meditation will be rendered futile.

Pursuing a profound state of tranquility and serenity serves as a commendable goal in its own right. However, the primary aim of this book is to enhance your concentration to the extent where you can manifest a distinct subjective reality through the practice of imaginative visualization. In order for this desired outcome to be realized, it is imperative that you possess a precise understanding of the alternate reality in which you envision yourself.

"What specific vision do you possess?" Please be cognizant of the following concerns, as it is quite effortless to aspire for "change" and ultimately find oneself in a more unfavorable predicament. Why? Lack of proper definition.

Each individual possesses aspirations and desires

It is essential for you to comprehend that the possession of hopes and wishes does not automatically translate into the possession of a personal vision. Hopes and aspirations alone do not suffice. Hopes and wishes generally encompass abstract sentiments of envisioning favorable transformation in the times ahead or desiring positive occurrences to manifest in one's life through unspecified means.

Although I can certainly comprehend and empathize with your sentiments regarding the high emotional intensity associated with hope and longing, it is imperative that you do not solely fixate on the transient sense of relief experienced when hoping and wishing for an improved reality. Given that we must confront the reality, it can be observed that a majority of individuals possess desires and aspirations, but regrettably lack the ability to enact significant transformations in their lives. Why? The mere existence of hopes and wishes does not suffice.

When individuals engage in hopes and aspirations, they are essentially indulging in fanciful musings. They are primarily seeking respite from their everyday vexations. They are aware of their discontentment. They are aware of the necessity for a transformation in their lives, thus they anticipate and aspire for the advent of favorable circumstances. They hold intentions and aspirations for a transformative improvement in their lives, often within an unattainable timeframe, thereby solely experiencing a temporary emotional relief arising from the overwhelming feelings of discouragement or even despair stemming from their present circumstances.

After experiencing the pleasurable sensation of release, they cease their actions. The act of hoping and wishing alone fails to incite them into genuine action or persuade them to reevaluate their mindsets, which subsequently hampers any meaningful change in their behavior. The underlying cause is their search for a form of emotional release. It is imperative to emphasize the significance of cultivating a distinct personal vision for oneself. A personal vision can be likened to possessing an emotional and psychological navigational guide.

In the absence of a cartographic tool and navigational device, one would find oneself in a state of disorientation.

Even in the absence of a map and compass, if you appear to be progressing, you are still disoriented. You are essentially engaged in a cycle of repetitive actions without clear indications of the progress being achieved. It is uncertain whether or not you are approaching or advancing further towards your desired destination. You have no clue. You are merely proceeding mechanically.

Please note that you are making a significant effort. You are actively taking measures, which is why you are proceeding by placing one foot ahead of the other. However, in the absence of proper navigational tools such as a map and compass, the execution of such activity becomes futile as it lacks direction and coherence, rendering the individual's efforts futile. Essentially, being unguided leads to aimlessness. The cultivation of a personal vision equips individuals with a navigational framework, providing them with the means to transform their desired alternate reality into their present existence.

To put it concisely, when one simplifies their personal vision, they effectively elucidate it to the degree that it functions analogously to a navigational aid encompassing both a map and a compass. It is exceedingly challenging to experience a sense of confusion or uncertainty when one possesses a clearly defined and well-articulated personal vision. May I inquire as to the method by which this task is executed? What is the process for constructing an individual vision that effectively steers you in the correct direction and allows you to evaluate your actions in a manner that propels you towards your overarching objectives, rather than futilely expending effort? Here's how.

Assume the role of a journalist

To commence the process of establishing your personal vision, it is imperative to regard it as a enigma of sorts. Journalists and investigators excel in unraveling enigmatic phenomena. Their intellectual superiority does not account for their success; rather, it can be attributed to their diligent adherence to a well-structured system and methodology. If you desire to precisely establish your personal vision, adopt the perspective of a journalist and inquire about the five W's and one H, which are commonly employed by reporters.

The quintessential components encompassed by the five W's are none other than the aspects pertaining to the identification of individuals, delineation of events or circumstances, determination of timing, specification of location, and discerning the underlying reasons or motivations. The letter H represents the concept of 'how'. Now, I request that you carefully consider your aspirations, desires, and any additional concepts pertaining to an alternate existence that you envision for your own life. Just know yourself out. Enumerate the alternative lifestyles that you would prefer to experience. To what extent would your present lifestyle substantially deviate from the alternative being considered? Direct your attention solely to these alternate options.

Now that you have documented your preliminary ideas, the subsequent phase entails delineating the individuals associated with your envisioned life and subsequently outlining the specific attributes and characteristics that characterize your desired existence. The aforementioned principle applies to the geographical location of the alternate reality that you aspire to manifest in your life. At what point in time would you prefer for all of these events to transpire? Is it realistic? Are there any subordinate objectives or supplementary time limits in place?

Ultimately, it is crucial to contemplate the underlying rationale for this particular visionary concept. Why not something else? This might pose some difficulty, as it requires you to be entirely truthful with yourself in this situation. Are you seeking an alternative version of reality that aligns with the desires of others? Do you regularly view numerous videos featuring gentlemen aboard luxurious yachts or private jets, and have you personally expressed the aspiration for such a lifestyle? Alternatively, are you merely acquiescing or assimilating the desires of others? It is imperative that it belongs to you. It must be comprehensible to you.

You are obligated to inquire about the reasons behind your actions and scrutinize your motivations, in order to gain a profound understanding of the precise alternative reality that you should earnestly pursue.

Ultimately, it is imperative to inquire about the methodology employed.

Contemplate the matter with utmost realism and inquire within yourself, "How can I effectively transform this personal vision into actuality?" For instance, supposing your personal vision entails residing in a luxurious abode valued at $6 million within the prominent Hollywood hills, it is evident that procuring the necessary financial resources marks the initial milestone. I am not solely referring to the financial aspect of purchasing the house, but rather emphasizing the necessity of obtaining the means to cover the expenses including property tax, maintenance costs, and other associated expenditures involved in the overall ownership of said property.

You need to consider within these parameters. Do not solely fixate on the luxurious automobile, the extravagant holiday, the grand residence, or the impeccable physique that you diligently craft in the fitness center purely for personal gratification. Additionally, pay attention to the means by which you will reach your destination. Upon thorough consideration, it becomes evident that the concept of "how" is essentially centered around the process of meticulously mapping out the path from point B - the ultimate destination of your vision - to point A - your current position. One must simply retrace their steps from the final destination. It is imperative that you consistently ask yourself the question of how, repeatedly, to ensure that no step is overlooked.

One cannot make any daring assumptions. It is imperative to maintain a high level of realism while progressing from the ultimate objective or ultimate aspiration to your present position. In a broader context, should your aspirations encompass leading a prosperous life replete with various material acquisitions, it becomes imperative to devise means of generating the necessary financial resources and subsequently engage in a reverse planning exercise to distinctly outline the requisite steps.

As an illustration, revisiting the mansion scenario, it would be necessary to generate a sum of $6 million in addition to approximately $2 million for supplementary expenses, resulting in a total of $8 million. What is your plan for generating the necessary funds? Subsequently, you can contemplate your present actions. Maybe you design websites. Rather than creating designs for others, perhaps it would be prudent for you to commence developing profit-generating websites for your own benefit. Therefore, one begins with the sum of $8 million and proceeds to analyze the number of income-generating websites that would be necessary to generate said amount, as well as the duration of time required for such endeavors, and so forth.

What you are currently engaged in is utilizing the term 'how' as a means to systematically dissect the various stages that separate your present reality from the envisioned and desired state of an ideal life. This is the methodology to maintain realism. One cannot proceed with blind leaps of faith, expecting a fortuitous outcome where a randomly purchased lottery ticket reveals itself as the winning one overnight. That plan lacks a firm foundation. I trust that the matter is apparent.

It is imperative that you avoid any logical discrepancies. You cannot rely on the occurrence of miraculous events such as acquiring a multi-million dollar account without any effort or logical basis. Such a procedure is not in accordance with the established guidelines. That\\\'s not realistic. I do not assert that it does not occur. I am confident that such occurrences can be observed occasionally, yet it is not plausible to structure one's life based on the expectation of an extremely rare and unlikely event. Do you comprehend the essence of the matter at hand?

Once more, carefully examine your motivations.

At this juncture, it may be presumed that you have already developed a comprehensive personal aspiration. Before proceeding, it is imperative that you re-evaluate your underlying motivations to ensure they genuinely stem from personal conviction. It is important to establish a clear understanding that your pursuit of your personal vision is driven by a genuine desire to achieve it. This is not to suggest that you merely engage in an act of mimicking or strive to emulate the lives of others. It is imperative to articulate and establish that your motivation derives from factors that are inherently pertinent and uniquely applicable to your personal circumstances.

Comprehend the ramifications of your desires.

Once you have identified and focused on your personal vision and established a relatively clear trajectory from your current situation to the desired outcome, the subsequent endeavor involves comprehending the ramifications and consequences associated with this vision. It is quite another matter to harbor a inclination towards acquiring a luxurious Mercedes Benz or a prestigious Ferrari. It is an entirely distinct matter to attain a comprehensive understanding of the extent of sacrifices and diligent efforts required to procure those possessions.

Comprehend the ramifications of your vision as it elicits a rather uncomplicated query. Are you prepared to dedicate the necessary time, effort, and willingness to make that vision a reality? How strong is your desire for it? Do you comprehend the extent of the efforts required to attain that alternate reality? It is imperative that this is made evident to you, as without implications, your understanding would be confined to a well-defined fantasy. Implications play a crucial role in acknowledging that certain obligations will be expected from you.

Repeated encounters with failure and setbacks will be necessary before ultimately prevailing. It would necessitate your display of patience. It would necessitate the allocation of your time and resources. It necessitates a willingness to forgo leisurely pursuits such as socializing with acquaintances and idling away time, in order to dedicate extensive hours to work and procure the financial capital needed to establish a company that holds the potential to realize your aspirations. Are you able to comprehend the functioning of this? Implications are crucial. It is imperative to complete this step, as it provides crucial information regarding the price you will be required to pay.

Final reminder

I would like to provide you with this ultimate reminder. Based on their apparent correlation, it can be deduced that the preceding step is indeed the final one. However, prior to concluding our discourse, it is imperative for me to provide you with this ultimate reminder. It is of utmost importance to meticulously delineate and precisely articulate one's personal vision, ensuring complete clarity and comprehensive understanding of its intricate particulars. It is essential to not only possess a well-crafted roadmap leading from your present state to your desired future, but also to thoroughly comprehend the ramifications of your aspirations and be prepared to endure the associated sacrifices.

Without undertaking that particular action, one can only engage in mere idle fanciful thoughts. You are purely indulging in hope and wishful thinking. Indeed, your aspirations and desires are well articulated and easily comprehensible. However, it is regrettably apparent that without a genuine emotional commitment to exert the necessary effort and endure the required sacrifices and diligent labor for an extended period of time, the realization of your dreams is unlikely to materialize.

There must exist a moment of dedication. There must exist an authentic emotional essence. By way of explanation, it is inadequate to simply state, "I am willing to engage in these various tasks." Put differently, such a declaration merely represents a cognitive acknowledgement. That's not enough. It is imperative for it to evoke emotions. It must be deeply ingrained in your heart and mind that, "I am determined to embark on this journey." It is expected to feature intricate twists and turns. It shall experience fluctuations in both directions. The path ahead is anticipated to be challenging, potentially requiring sacrifices and enduring discomfort; however, I wish to highlight a notable aspect. The value of my dream is significant. I am prepared to provide the necessary compensation.

Such is the emotional state that one must strive to attain. Otherwise, you\\\'re not visualizing. Alternatively, you would merely be relying on mere speculation and desire. There is a difference between daydreaming for emotional escape and actual creative visualization. Let this distinction serve as your guide. The disparity, undoubtedly, lies in comprehending the ramifications and demonstrating the willingness to be cognizant of not just the intellectual aspects, but also experiencing it at an emotional depth.

Dreaming For Others

Regrettably, we do not have authority over the lives of others. While it is understandable that one may desire their prosperity to extend to their entire family, it is advisable to prioritize one's individual desires rather than assuming the collective aspirations of the family unit. It is advisable to promote the adoption of visualization techniques among other family members, as you may discover that your collective pursuit of solutions aligns harmoniously. The argument being presented is that while you may envision a romantic relationship with a particular individual of the opposite gender, there is no certainty that their sentiments will align with yours. Enhancing your potential in the company of that individual is possible by personal development, although facilitating the fulfillment of their dreams may not be within your control.

You might possess qualities that make you an ideal match for your current partner, however, in the event that you aspire for a relationship with someone else, the most effective approach is to enhance your own attributes and hope that they become aware of your qualities. You are unable to influence the perspectives of others merely out of a strong desire for a particular outcome.

"Let us examine certain self-esteem concerns that cannot be remedied using the method demonstrated:

Should I conjure an image of his eternal affection towards me, it remains subject to uncertainties beyond my control, as destiny plays a role in shaping such outcomes.

If I possess autonomy over my own fate, what was the reason for his departure? Furthermore, you are not able to speak on behalf of others.

Individuals who find themselves in a deteriorating relationship frequently assume the burden of responsibility for the dissolution. They instantaneously surmise that there must be some inherent flaw within themselves for the relationship to result in failure. Nevertheless, existence does not unfold in such a manner. While you may possess qualities that make you an ideal partner in the eyes of some individuals, it is important to acknowledge that if your current partner is on the verge of ending the relationship, attempting to modify yourself will not resolve the predicament. It is highly likely that there exists an issue within the relationship itself, rather than solely with one or both individuals involved. Cease your efforts to rectify matters and redirect your focus towards the utmost cultivation of your own character. Numerous individuals experience the disconcerting realization of encountering a former spouse whom they no longer recognize following a divorce. The rationale behind this phenomenon stems from individuals adapting and modifying their lives to accommodate one another. They were not obliged to undertake such action, yet they proceeded regardless, thereby altering their very essence. It is scarcely astonishing, therefore, that following seven years of matrimony, their spouse found themselves disillusioned with their partner, consequently leading to a sense of self-estrangement. Each person is interdependent. When two individuals encounter one another and develop romantic feelings, it should not be assumed that their subsequent relationship would diminish the importance of one person over the other. Look at these phrases. These statements are frequently made, but individuals who employ visualization are advised to refrain from them.

It seemed as though we were in perfect unity, yet it is evident that you were a distinctly separate individual.
I became so engrossed in his companions that I unintentionally disregarded my own acquaintances. It is not surprising that you are experiencing feelings of solitude.

Your focus should revolve around the core essence of your being, the pursuits you aspire to undertake in your life, and the manner in which you wish to portray yourself. Once individuals attentively focus on personal growth and align themselves with their desired self-image, subsequent achievements shall naturally ensue, obviating the need for inauthentic self-transformation.

It is possible that you are pursuing the same aspiration. It is plausible that you share identical mental imagery. It is possible that you and your partner could engage in collective meditation, wherein you both focus on the same mental imagery, thereby enhancing the manifestation of your respective aspirations simultaneously. Nevertheless, it is crucial to recognize that the potential you possess within yourself serves as a means to pursue your own aspirations and desires in life, rather than solely aiming to satisfy the wishes of others, whose aspirations may or may not align with your own.

Why Do People Use Visualization Techniques?

The utmost challenge pertaining to any endeavor, acquisition, or recourse, whether it pertains to our desires or necessities, lies in cultivating belief.

For instance, we may seek alternative employment in order to enhance our financial situation, or we may aspire to pursue a different vocation due to encountering unfavorable circumstances in our present professional capacity.

We may perceive them as dull and desire something more stimulating and intellectually demanding.

Cognitive exercises activate the implicated neural pathways. It regulates our instinctual response to stimuli, triggering an escalation in heart rate, elevation in blood pressure, and intensification of respiration.

When mentally visualizing the movements alone, it triggers nervous system responses akin to those observed during the actual execution of the corresponding physical action.

Although it may appear fantastical, certain studies have proposed that the act of visualization possesses the potential to facilitate the achievement of desired outcomes, even in the absence of any physical effort.

When one engages in frequent acts of visualization, it is likely that their neural processes will adapt in a manner that facilitates a sense of familiarity when actually performing said actions. It appears as though you are delineating a pathway within the nervous system.

What Is The Functioning Mechanism Of Visualization Techniques?

The potential reasons and mechanism underlying the failure of this visualization predominantly arise when we contemplate its efficacy. Generating disillusionment regarding the efficacy of visualization is a rather effortless endeavor, irrespective of the frequency or intensity with which we concentrate on anticipating the outcome. Our yearning for it to come to fruition persists regardless.

The concept of using thought visualization as a method to enhance one's life has become largely accepted and ingrained within our society.

Subsequently, rather than seeking to acquire knowledge and understanding about the possible reasons for its malfunction, we invariably abandon the situation and relinquish our pursuit, thereby perpetuating a lifestyle in which the realization of our considerable capabilities becomes unattainable.

In contemporary society, numerous renowned athletes incorporate creative visualization as an integral component of their training regimen.

It is imperative that we do not overlook the fact that visualization is indeed the desired outcome that we seek, and it will materialize in due course.

In our daily lives, there are alternative approaches to enhance our ability to run distances of 1-2 miles at a faster pace. Specifically, dedicating one hour out of the four days in a week to visualizing the act of running these miles more swiftly can potentially yield greater results.

Although daydreaming can certainly be beneficial when it comes to manifesting our goals or desires.

By adhering to a dependable timetable and allocating regular, scheduled intervals specifically dedicated to engaging in creative visualization, one can reasonably expect to achieve significantly enhanced outcomes.

Chapter One: Identifying Personal Aspirations and Life Goals

I frequently inquire with individuals who assert that their aspirations and ambitions consistently fail to materialize. The reality is that there exists a distinct justification for this. I inquire about the aforementioned aspirations and ambitions, and frequently find that individuals tend to portray them using imprecise language.

- My aspiration is to acquire substantial wealth.
- I aspire to achieve success.
- I desire to acquire my ideal residence
- I aspire to possess my envisioned abode • I yearn for my perfect dwelling • I long to obtain my dream house • I am determined to achieve my desired home

I aspire to acquire my desired vehicle

These aspirations are intended for individuals who engage in idle fantasizing. These dreams lack authenticity and tangibility, as the individuals I conversed with had a rather abstract perception of them, devoid of concrete understanding. It is imperative to articulate clear and concise aspirations, as without a defined destination in mind, it becomes exceedingly challenging to successfully navigate towards it. Let us consider one of these alternatives. The aspiration to acquire wealth can be contemplated from various perspectives. A hungry child would experience an overwhelming sense of affluence upon receiving a ten-dollar banknote. Having an adequate financial means to cover expenses without any apprehension may be deemed satisfactory by certain individuals. Although the act of winning the lottery may bring joy to others, without a concrete plan or blueprint, it remains an abstract dream with uncertain prospects of realization.

To initiate the process of visualization, it is imperative to delineate your life's aspirations through meticulous note-taking and comprehensive strategizing, thereby enabling you to effectively envision the realization of your goals. If you desire a particular automobile, refrain from indulging in idle fantasies and procure accurate information regarding the financial implications of owning said vehicle. Make your plan real. Subsequently, you may initiate the process of altering your mindset so as to transcend mere contemplation of your desired actions, but rather commence their execution.

Frequently, individuals approach me with inadequately formulated ideas that are destined to fail due to their incomplete nature. They lack self-belief as much as they lack faith in their aspirations, thereby traversing through life in a state of wishing rather than existing. That's a huge difference. Allow me to elucidate the distinction before you delve deeper into this literary work.

Existence entails having faith in one's actions. When a child assumes the role of an astronaut, his intent is not to merely express a desire to become an astronaut, but rather to assert his identity as an astronaut. The inherent imaginative capacities of a child enable proficient visualization, as the child remains unaffected by societal constraints that might diminish his aspirations. He embodies his own aspirations.

Now look at adults. Their perspectives are initially shaped by the influence of their parents.

It is not permissible to engage in this activity.
It is prohibited to engage in such actions.
• Conform to my instructions regarding your behavior • Abide by the guidelines I provide for your conduct • Adhere to the directives I give you in terms of how

you should behave ● Observe the instructions I provide and exhibit the prescribed behavior

Subsequently, they are further influenced by their peers.

● You are an individual of admirable qualities.

● That attire is inappropriate for the prom.

● It is impossible for you to gain weight. It appears that your opinions have been shaped by the impact of social media and magazines.

You do not exude coolness if you happen to be overweight.

● If you do not possess good companions, you are devoid of something essential.

● Your current hairstyle does not meet the desired criteria ● Your hair style does not conform to the required standard ● Your hair does not match the preferred style ● The style of your hair does not align with the prescribed standards

In conclusion, one's character is ultimately shaped by the cumulative impact of various influences. Now direct your attention towards the child. The child remains as the astronaut. Each individual possesses an inherent capacity to realize their desired potential, yet life's adversities often diminish this innate ability. Consequently, as adults, many succumb to these setbacks and relinquish their aspirations. Individuals who do not possess the opportunity to freely express their identities and aspirations cannot be considered fortunate. They are merely embodying their desired identities, for it is their deliberate decision to assertively safeguard their aspirations from any encumbrances.

Please take a moment to sit down and contemplate your true identity, using a physical paper as a tool for introspection. It is not a matter of what you aspire to become, but rather a revelation of your true essence beneath all facades.

- I am financially affluent and have the luxury of being able to take vacations at my discretion.
- I highly advocate nurturing positive relationships • I promote the cultivation of healthy friendships • I endorse the development of constructive social bonds • I recommend fostering positive connections with others • I support the establishment of beneficial friendships
- I am an accomplished musician patiently waiting in the wings for my grand entrance.

Nurture That Image

Once you have formulated your life's vision, it is imperative to cultivate and sustain it. Just as a plant requires nurturing, it is essential to tend to your vision in order for it to develop within your cognitive framework. Cultivating your vision necessitates relinquishing the negative perceptions that have persisted within you for a considerable duration.

Initially, it is imperative to secure a serene and secluded environment in which you can effectively contemplate the mental imagery held within your mind. It may either be situated in your bedroom or an exterior location. If feasible, locate a setting devoid of any disruptions.

Furthermore, commence the process of visualizing this image mentally. Envision intricate and precise visuals. If your objective entails embarking on the long-desired vacation to the Caribbean, envisage yourself strolling along the pristine white sand, indulging in a refreshing swim in the azure sea, and luxuriating under the gentle caress of the sun's radiant warmth. Strive to enhance the clarity of the mental image.

Furthermore, maintain the belief that you have already achieved it. This constitutes the pivotal aspect in the realm of visualization. It is imperative to employ mental strategies that deceive oneself into perceiving the envisioned goal as already achieved. You must cultivate a mindset that convinces your consciousness of having already accomplished the task at hand.

Furthermore, unleash the positive emotions harbored within you. When one derives pleasure from their envisioned mental imagery and firmly holds the belief that it has already been achieved, those emotions will manifest themselves. In the event of such an occurrence, endeavor to sustain the aforementioned positive sentiment for a duration of no less than one minute.

Do this regularly. It is recommended to engage in this activity twice daily, allocating a minimum of 10-15 minutes each time. Persistent mental imagery dismantles existing cognitive frameworks and substitutes them with fresh ones. If you have consistently displayed a pessimistic demeanor throughout your entire existence, it is improbable for this disposition to be abruptly eradicated through a single occurrence of visualization. It is essential to maintain regularity in order to disrupt the habitual pattern.

Dismiss the pessimistic thoughts that reside within your mind. If you engage in visualization for a brief duration, only to be plagued by pessimistic thoughts throughout the remainder of the day, this practice will undeniably prove detrimental to your overall well-being.

Children possess a remarkable aptitude for visualization, evident in their imaginative role-playing. In the film "Up," Carl and Ellie manifest their aspiration by assuming the roles of explorers. It is not surprising that research indicates a positive correlation between advanced imaginative play in children and higher levels of intelligence.

Action Point:

Please make a note of the scheduled time and location for your visualization session.

_____

_____

_____

Once you have indicated the specific time and location, demonstrate your commitment to carry it out. Initially, it may present some difficulties, but with consistent repetition, it eventually becomes ingrained as a customary behavior.

INTRODUCTION

Design Mind for Data Visualization is a literary work that primarily centers around elucidating the cognitive aspects of visual perception prior to delving into the intricate details involved in its fabrication. This book imparts knowledge on the subject of visual perception, information design, and the essential elements and principles that must be employed to craft a compelling data visualization. If by chance you have encountered this literary work, there are three compelling rationales that may persuade you to perseverate and peruse its content:

You are considerably daunted by the sophisticated designs crafted by your colleagues and possess an absolute dearth of expertise in the realm of graphic design.
You require an infusion of inspiration to elevate the quality of your work.
You are facing challenges in capturing the attention of your audience with regards to your graphs and are in urgent need of assistance.

Fortunately, this literary piece possesses the potential to assist you in addressing all three quandaries. Creating a visualization does not require exceptional expertise, and a graph or chart can be effortlessly arranged by anyone. However, does your audience establish a meaningful connection with your work? Do you take pride in the final output of your design work? If you aspire to create extraordinary visualizations, this book will prove invaluable in guiding you along your path. It aspires to assist individuals who seek to enhance the aesthetics, relevance, inclusivity, and emotional impact of their visualizations. Furthermore, it provides a comprehensive breakdown of the entire process involved in generating, crafting, and interpreting a visualization, thus enabling you to undertake design initiatives with prudence and discernment.

The initial segment of this literary work, entitled 'Eyes, Brains, and Hearts, Oh My', is dedicated to exploring the scientific aspects pertaining to perception. What is the manner in which individuals perceive and process visual information? The process of visual perception and information retention is impaired when an individual gazes upon your graphic. It extensively investigates the profound impact of that process on design considerations. The passage primarily emphasizes the importance of acquiring a comprehensive comprehension of human perception in design, as this knowledge greatly aids in the development of data visualizations that are inclusive, efficient, and informative.

The subsequent section of this literary work, titled "Elements and Principles of Design," commences by introducing fundamental principles in graphic design, intended to guide readers from a state of design detachment towards a state of design acumen. It places emphasis on the fundamental elements necessary to construct a stimulating and aesthetically captivating design. After becoming acquainted with fundamental concepts such as line, shape, balance, contrast, and layout, you will develop the ability to discern visual elements and incorporate these essential design principles into your future endeavors. By carefully and strategically incorporating these elements and principles, one can craft a visually captivating representation that conveys profound meaning.

The third and paramount section of the book, titled "Apply Your Design Mind to Data Visualization," centers on the practical application of the accumulated knowledge from the preceding parts, enabling the seamless integration of such insights into your forthcoming designs. It provides comprehensive insights into the precise techniques employed in crafting a proficient visualization by leveraging the core principles underlying information design. In the third section, I elaborate on the methodology of developing a personalized workflow and constructing a comprehensive data visualization style manual, which serves to uphold uniformity across all project endeavors. In addition, I delve into establishing an efficient design methodology that will enhance productivity and minimize the occurrence of revision. This portion of the book also centers its attention on the notions of accessibility, diversity, and inclusion within the realm of design. Given that the fundamental tenet of design revolves around understanding one's target demographic and accommodating their preferences and requirements, the book persuasively encourages the reader to exhaustively explore various empathetic avenues prior to embarking upon the design process.

As a data author, it is imperative to present your data narrative in a manner that effectively conveys the highest level of information while minimizing any potential for confusion. Design constitutes the act of visually conveying information, and your visual representation should strive to educate, persuade, or amuse your audience without necessitating verbalization on your part. It would pose a greater challenge to accomplish this task without taking into account the viewpoint of your audience during the design phase. This task entails a substantial level of accountability. Designing impactful and meaningful visualizations is contingent only upon comprehending the identity of the individuals involved and the motivations behind their actions. Prior to commencing the design process and determining the manner in which it shall be executed, it is imperative to possess a comprehensive understanding of the intended audience for whom the design is intended. Every single procedure is meticulously described, as it is imperative for the acquisition of visual language proficiency and aptitudes to be closely intertwined with comprehending visual impairments, international spectators, human cognition, and sentiment.

Ultimately, the concluding segment of the book, entitled "Progressing Towards the Future," presents methodologies to stimulate and sustain the coursing of your imaginative faculties. Emerging advancements, evolving preferences, shifting requirements, and fluctuating fashions exhibit a propensity for swift transformation. Therefore, to attain triumph as a data author, one must wholeheartedly embrace this pursuit with unwavering commitment, fervor, and ardor. The pursuit of knowledge in design is an ongoing, never-ending endeavor that demands continual examination, application, and exploration of the intricate workings of the human psyche. By utilizing this book as your mentor, you will unlock boundless possibilities for your artistic prowess and gain profound wisdom in a domain that will continuously engage and exhilarate you.

This book has been authored with extensive research, profound insights, and unwavering commitment to assist proficient data analysts who seek to elevate their skills in a creative manner, and who currently find themselves unstimulated or disengaged. In addition, it will serve as a valuable resource for individuals passionate about data visualization who seek to enhance their professional portfolios, as well as those seeking straightforward and effective design solutions to enhance their presentations and visualizations in a professional setting. This volume serves as a valuable resource for individuals grappling with the challenge of commencing their design endeavors. It will provide you with a comprehensive comprehension of fundamental design principles, enabling you to enhance your mental design repertoire and effectively apply this knowledge to your data visualizations. It elucidates the significance of deliberating over dimensions, form, and juxtaposition to capture one's attention, devising a framework in a manner that avoids excessive dominance, crafting designs infused with empathy, and various other aspects. The book will provide readers with a fresh outlook on viewing the world and comprehending the extensive potential of the digital audience. It imparts the value of conscientious design and the creation of impactful experiences aimed at eliciting positive emotional responses from viewers. By embarking on the process of self-exploration in the field of design, you embark upon a transformative voyage towards unleashing your latent creative abilities, aiming to create data visualizations that not only engage the intellect but also deeply resonate with the emotions.

Affirmation

The affirmation stage constitutes the third element of the creative visualization process. An affirmation entails providing a declaration that verifies the truthfulness of a given matter. Affirmations are commonly referred to as mantras. This method has been utilized by spiritual mystics throughout history, constituting a significant component within the creative visualization methodology.

Upon envisioning your ideal existence, it is imperative to assert and validate its reality. It is recommended to perform this immediately following the process of visualization. Presented herewith are several guidelines delineating the process of formulating one's personal affirmation.

It is imperative that one utilizes the present tense when formulating affirmations. It is not advisable to express sentiments such as "I will attain wealth in the future" or "I will acquire self-assurance eventually." You are required to acknowledge that you have indeed attained your objectives. Express something in a manner reflecting formality: "Phrase such as "My existence is replete with blessings" or "I possess unwavering assurance in my aptitude and competence." The utilization of the present tense when crafting affirmations shall prompt the subconscious mind to perceive these declarations as factual, in turn, prompting it to empower and motivate oneself towards undertaking actions conducive to the realization of aspirations and objectives."

It is imperative to experience a positive emotional response – Repeat a self-affirmation and attentively gauge the resulting feelings. Do you experience a sense of joy when you express it, or does it induce a feeling of unease? Certain individuals experience discomfort when expressing the affirmation "I possess great wealth" or "I am a person of substantial financial means." If an affirmation causes unease, consider rephrasing it. Rather than stating "I am a millionaire", it would be more appropriate to articulate it as "I lead a life of affluence." It is worth noting that your subconscious mind is not solely influenced by visual representations, but also by emotions and sensations.

Maintain a pleasant countenance - A smile can be of great assistance when expressing affirmation. Elicit a sense of joy and affection.

71

Let go - Following the process of affirming and visualizing, relinquish control to the universe, exhibiting faith that it will diligently work towards manifesting your aspirations.

Concerning Manifesting

Verbal expressions can be employed in various manners depending on the given context. In accordance with our intentions, the concept of manifesting our wishes, objectives, and desires that materialize within our thoughts could be deemed as "showing up" in the context of our usage. Unfortunately, this will not grant you the authority to exercise control over other individuals, as such dominion over others is unattainable. Every individual was presented with an opportunity to exercise their independent will, and it is imperative that we seize this chance to make deliberate decisions in order to reach our utmost potential.

Displaying presence serves as a means of motivating us. It empowers us to seize command over our lives rather than simply leaving it to chance and fate. It confers upon us the ability to transform our ideas into genuine manifestations that are meaningful and valuable to us.

If you continue to contemplate financial matters, a mental image of currency or a financial instrument will inevitably arise. This will undoubtedly prove to be a valuable experience for you in the present day.

One may observe a dollar displayed on a signage or engage in a conversation pertaining to financial matters. In general, if one merely observes or becomes cognizant of something without possessing it, it proves futile. You may also consider employing alternative methods to actualize it.

Attendance serves as a gift meant to actualize our aspirations, yet it may become counterproductive if we fail to carefully deliberate on what we intend to manifest. We can attend an event or engage in an activity even if it is not our preference, as long as we maintain the mental representation of that particular item or concept.

Every individual possesses the inherent ability to manifest their aspirations effortlessly in their life. It is simply that we were not educated in this truth during our formative years, and we were inundated with a great deal of information that has caused us to overlook our innate ability to manifest and attract. The fact of the matter is that we are each exerting control with this power, although it may be latent within you. With this established comprehension, coupled with a fervent pursuit, an attending regimen... maybe stirred up.

Whichever aspect you choose to give prominence to, you are manifesting it into your life with greater speed than you may perceive. If you consistently focus on what you wish to avoid thinking, feeling, or encountering, it will become evident that this is precisely what you are manifesting.

Through the exploration of these age-old techniques of appearance, you possess the capacity to maintain unwavering attention, calmness, and concentration on your desired thoughts, emotions, and encounters. From this particular geographical point, one shall discover that their utmost aspirations and desires shall manifest and become a tangible reality in their sphere of existence.

Manifestation is a remarkable gift, imbued with the potential to fulfill our deepest desires as well as alleviate our greatest concerns. Therefore, it is crucial to employ it judiciously ...

The Law Of Attraction

We reside within a Cosmos regulated by imperceptible principles. These intangible entities elude our perception and physical interaction, yet they continually manifest themselves in the backdrop of our existence. These laws, without any deviation, operate uniformly for all individuals and can be categorized into two distinct groups.

The initial set of laws pertains to the physical realm. The physical laws dictate the functioning of our material realm. The laws that follow are commonly referred to as metaphysical laws.

The metaphysical laws preside over the realm of our internal reality, shaping and projecting our inner musings onto the elements that constitute our external, tangible world. The metaphysical laws serve as a mirror, reflecting our thoughts, words, and emotions directed towards our own selves.

We possess a greater understanding of the fundamental principles governing the physical phenomena in the universe. As an illustration, the Law of Gravity serves as a prime example.

The Law of Gravity eludes visual or tactile apprehension, yet its existence is undeniably discernible. All individuals and entities, without exception, adhere to this principle. Gravity tethers us to the Earth. Gravity maintains the temporal synchronization of tides, the positional stability of celestial bodies, and the rotational motion of the solar system.

There is no need for one to activate the Law of Gravity; by simply relinquishing one's grasp on an object, it will naturally descend to the ground.

A further illustration of a physical principle is represented by the Law of Centrifugal Force. One cannot evade this law, for in the event that one drives excessively fast around a bend, it is highly probable that their vehicle will end up in the adjacent ravine.

These laws exhibit a sense of impartiality, rendering them universally applicable. They neither bestow rewards nor inflict punishments; they solely exist. Physical laws exhibit impartiality. The Law of Electricity applies to both the surgeon and the criminal who employ electricity for their respective purposes.

While the devastating impact of hurricanes, typhoons, or tornadoes may not be preferable, it is important to recognize that they play a significant role in maintaining planetary temperature and sustaining abundant life.

Electricity has been accessible to humanity since our earliest habitation of caves; however, its integration into our shared understanding only occurred following our comprehension of the principles governing electricity and its practical application. Currently, we are in the process of comprehending the methodologies required to access and harness metaphysical principles, including the law of attraction.

Metaphysical laws have been in existence for a significant period of time. Metaphysics was imparted by erudite individuals including scholars, priests, and philosophers, with its origins traceable to the ancient mystery schools of Egypt and the Druids.

Amidst the celestial expanse, the Druids would reverently proclaim, "In concordance with celestial occurrences, thus corresponds the terrestrial realm." With profound insight, the Druids comprehended the profound significance and profound interconnection of the phrase "in semblance to the heavens" (the realm of thought) and "in resonance with the earth" (the physical plane). This fundamental principle remains as valid in the present day as it was during its initial articulation.

Just over one hundred years ago, the principles of the New Thought movement were disseminated by esteemed organizations such as Theosophy societies and noteworthy

American Transcendentalists, including Ralph Waldo Emerson, Henry David Thoreau, and their contemporaries. As these concepts took shape, they gradually coalesced into organized belief systems, one of which is the faith I adhere to known as Religious Science.

Ernest Holmes, the esteemed pioneer of the Church of Religious Science, was counted among the venerated figures of the New Thought movement. He authored The Science of Mind, which encompassed the principles of the law of attraction. His book provides valuable insights and elucidates the dynamics of the conscious and subconscious mind, thereby presenting a comprehensive understanding of how we can exert influence over the physical realm using the principles of this scientific discipline.

In the year 2006, the Law of Attraction gained significant prominence courtesy of author Rhonda Byrne, who achieved widespread recognition for her publication titled The Secret. Currently, a vast range of literary works, audio recordings, guided practices, and compact discs pertaining to the phenomenon of the Law of Attraction are readily accessible.

The Law of Attraction is commonly regarded as a form of mystical transmutation. When integrated into our daily existence, it shall manifest any aspiration from the ethereal realm into our tangible reality. Nevertheless, grasping the intricacies of the Law of Attraction is not as straightforward as simply reciting a handful of affirmations and anticipating instant outcomes.

The intricacies of the Law of Attraction lie within the myriad of factors where ancillary laws intersect.

As an example, the Law of Attraction operates in conjunction with other legal principles such as the Law of Vibration, the Law of Cause and Effect, and the Law of Correspondence. In order for your aspiration to be realized, it is imperative that all these laws are brought into conformity.

The principle of Correspondence is intricately connected to the vibrational energy that emanates from within you. The principle of correspondence establishes that the mental image you possess is reflected in the corresponding events and circumstances that manifest in your life.

According to the words of Christ in King James Version Matthew 18:19, he proclaimed, "Moreover, I solemnly declare to you that if two individuals on earth come to a mutual agreement concerning any matter they may request, it shall be accomplished for them by my heavenly Father."

Numerous belief systems interpret this concept as referring to the collective prayer of two or more individuals. Although I acknowledge the possibility, I contend that it is actually the rational intellect and the subjective emotional force. Indeed, manifestation will only take place when your desires are aligned with the expression of your emotions.

It is crucial that your thoughts, words, and energy are congruent. As an example, it is possible to possess a rational aspiration for financial prosperity, yet harbor a sense of inadequacy or unworthiness towards attaining it. Regardless of the extent of prayer, it will not manifest in your reality. The Universe, in its infinite capacity, unfailingly yields to the more dominant spectrum of human emotions.

Allow me to present one of my preferred illustrations that effectively exemplify this fundamental principle. The reasoning faculty rationalizes that it would be unwise to partake in consuming a donut due to one's commitment to a dietary regimen. Conversely, the innate sentiments resurface and vehemently demand indulgence in the gratifying act of consuming a donut, urging with a resounding exclamation of "Donut!" The emotions win. The force of emotions invariably triumphs.

If one desires the Law of Attraction to operate efficaciously in their life, it is imperative to grasp the mechanisms by which the Law of Attraction functions alongside other legal principles. Legislation such as the statute of vibration.

According to the principle of the Law of Vibration, all entities within the cosmos possess their distinct energetic vibrations.

The rocks, trees, and plants, although they may seem motionless, are in fact in a state of vibration. The energy possessed by rocks is characterized by its low density, resulting in imperceptible visible movement for individuals. Nevertheless, scientific research has corroborated that rocks, crystals, trees, mountains, and all other elements within our universe are in a state of continuous motion and vibration, albeit at different frequencies. As human beings, along with our fellow beings in the animal kingdom, we possess an elevated vibrational frequency.

Are you able to recollect the memorable sequence depicted in the film Jurassic Park, wherein the Tyrannosaurus Rex's foot made contact with the earth, resulting in the water within the glasses resonating while inside the vehicle along with the children? Our words exhibit identical characteristics. It resonates analogously with our cognitive processes. In addition, the utterances we articulate possess an inherent vibrational force encapsulated within every vowel and consonant.

In the realm of Hinduism and various eastern spiritual traditions, adherents commonly employ the sacred syllable, known as "Om," to enhance their vibrational frequencies during periods of prayer and meditation. The term 'Om' originates from the Sanskrit language and signifies the notions of 'source' or 'supreme' when translated. The chanting of the "om" serves to assess our vibrational frequency and energy, enabling us to harmonize and establish a spiritual connection with the Divine.

This vibrational energy operates in parallel with the Principle of Correspondence. For example, achieving a million-dollar lottery win is unlikely unless your energy or vibration is attuned to the magnitude of a million dollars. You will solely manifest within your personal encounters that which you hold to be true concerning your own identity. Your conscious and subconscious faculties will elicit the manifestation of the corresponding image in the physical realm.

Should you encounter challenges in accepting compliments, you may impede your progress in enhancing your financial prowess.

The efficacy of the Law of Attraction is impeded when it encounters an internal obstacle. These impediments manifest as emotions of inadequacy or the unfavorable notions one may harbor concerning oneself.

Aristotle was a highly esteemed Hellenic philosopher whose profound insights continue to be imparted in present-day academic institutions. He articulated that true understanding of a subject is only achieved once we comprehend its underlying rationale, or in other words, its causality. Moreover, he expounded upon these four fundamental causes with comprehensive elucidation within the pages of his renowned work, Metaphysics.

Aristotle, Jesus, and other revered religious and philosophical leaders all comprehended the principle of causality. A phenomenon observed in the physical realm is the occurrence of intense snowfall during winter seasons, which subsequently leads to the emergence of springtime flooding.

In the realm of metaphysics, you hold the primary agency for all occurrences within your life.

The beliefs one holds regarding their own self are liable to materialize in the realm of tangible reality. We actively participate in the process of creation alongside the divine, thus shaping our individual experiences.

According to the biblical verse found in Proverbs, 23:7, it is stated, "The disposition of a person is reflected by their thoughts and beliefs."

Ernest Holmes, in his literary work titled The Science of Mind, posits that existence functions as a reflective surface, wherein one's cognitions are reciprocated. Holmes meticulously elucidates the mechanism through which thoughts manifest as tangible entities.

Moreover, it is imperative to exercise caution and recognize the influence that your words carry. This holds particularly true when calling upon the influence of the phrase "I am" in your existence.

When Moses inquired about the name of God, God replied with the statement, "I am who I am." This can be found in the King James Version of the Bible, specifically in Exodus 3:14. You exercise this capability each time you utter the phrase, 'I am'. By uttering these words, you are essentially engaging in a process of co-creation alongside the divine entity known as God, who governs the Universe. When one declares, "I am unwell; I am financially disadvantaged; I am devoid of affection," one effectively attracts these negative circumstances into their personal reality. Rather than using the informal tone of "Instead, say," a more formal way to express the same idea could be: "Alternatively, one may express feelings of good health and abundance by stating, 'I possess excellent health and wealth is amassing; I emanate love, exhibit loving qualities, and am deserving of affection.'" By altering your thought patterns and the manner in which you articulate your self-perception, you have the ability to transform the external reality you encounter.

In subsequent sections, we shall delve into the realm of co-creation abilities. However, prior to undertaking this exploration, it is imperative to undertake the removal of any inhibitory thoughts, emotions, or past occurrences that have the potential to impede the manifestation of positive outcomes and hinder the achievement of your aspirations.

What Are The Reasons For Integrating Visualization Into One's Life, And What Is The Most Straightforward Approach To Embracing This Practice?

The practice of mental imagery holds the potential to yield triumph, and should you aspire to achieve true success in your existence, employing visualization may prove advantageous. A favorable mindset is imperative for achieving success in life as it fosters the cultivation of confidence and self-assurance. Maintaining a positive mindset will enhance your overall emotional state, as it allows for the enrichment of your life experience, thus mitigating the adverse impact of pessimistic thoughts on your well-being. The subsequent exercises presented herein are beneficial in fostering the cultivation of a constructive mindset:

Open your Mind

To cultivate a positive mindset, it is advisable to embrace a receptive mindset, fostering positivity and attentiveness to the perspectives of others. Comprehend their viewpoint, and demonstrate esteem for their thoughts, while embracing their proposals and critiques with a receptive mindset. Take heed of their ideas and thoughts to uncover boundless prospects for oneself.

Regularly compile a list of 10 things for which you express gratitude.

It is imperative that you consistently document ten elements that you express gratitude for each day. Developing a positive mindset will prove beneficial, allowing the opportunity for the rapid cultivation of an optimistic outlook. Engaging in this practice will cultivate a sense of gratitude towards the positive aspects that currently exist in your life. It is unnecessary to solely emphasize grand achievements, as even the smallest actions possess the potential to bring about significant transformations in one's life.

Develop a Consistent Practice of Meditation

Engaging in mindfulness practices can effectively distance oneself from negative influences and subsequently, contribute to an enhanced physical well-being. The practice of meditation holds equal value, independent of a person's spiritual beliefs or inclinations. It is imperative that you locate a tranquil and serene location in which to engage in meditation. One can engage in meditation within a tranquil space to minimize potential distractions. Direct your attention to constructive matters as you engage in various forms of meditative practices.

Strategies for Cultivating a Positive Self-Image

To cultivate self-esteem through the use of affirmations, it is imperative to direct your attention towards your abilities and areas of proficiency. It is unnecessary to fixate on one's flaws as doing so will impede progress. Do not be overly concerned about failures, as they can foster personal growth and development. It will facilitate a more favorable perception of oneself. Herein lie several constructive assertions for cultivating self-esteem:

My self-esteem is steadily increasing over time.

I acknowledge my loss and endeavor to examine its advantageous elements.

I place confidence in my capabilities.

I have the capability to accomplish any task.

I possess a robust sense of confidence and a strong level of self-esteem.

I am capable of attaining any goal in accordance with my desires.

I hold deep affection and unwavering confidence in my own being.

I acknowledge my capabilities.

I am able to communicate regarding my own positive thoughts.

I possess exceptional beauty and demonstrate a remarkable level of creativity.

Recognize and Address Negative Thoughts and Fears for Their Elimination

In the initial phase, it is essential to introspect and determine whether the predominant state of your mind throughout the day is characterized by negative or positive thoughts. In order to achieve this objective, it is necessary for you to ascertain negative thoughts. The commencement of negative thoughts is as follows:

Unable to accomplish" instead of "can.

Negative response is expected, rather than an affirmative one.

Lacking certainty instead of confident.

Unsuccessful outcome instead of achievement

If you are harboring these thoughts within your mind, regrettably, you are nourishing its negativity. The primary issue of contemporary times revolves around individuals being ensnared by their own thoughts. Frequently, you succumb to the power of your thoughts, rather than exerting control over them to yield advantageous outcomes for yourself. It is imperative that you acquire the ability to exercise control over your thoughts.

Underutilized Resources to Enhance Cognitive Capacity

The cultivation of psychological fortitude is crucial in managing the diverse challenges and complexities that arise throughout one's existence. There are primarily five factors that are frequently disregarded, including:

Confidence and belief

Capacity to conquer challenges.

Pain endurance capacity

The aspiration and resolve to persevere on your path.

The capacity to overcome apprehension

Confidence

Confidence serves as the bedrock of mental fortitude as it facilitates the attainment of excellence in any athletic endeavor. It is imperative that you maintain a steadfast belief in your aptitude to accomplish your objective. Should you believe that you lack the ability to attain your desired objectives, it shall result in your ultimate defeat, impeding your future progress. It is imperative to uphold self-belief, as exposure to any detrimental influences could potentially undermine one's confidence and exacerbate self-doubt. It is crucial to maintain the belief in your capacity to accomplish your objectives.

Overcome Adversity

Every individual inevitably encounters challenges at various points in their lives, and for certain individuals, these circumstances may prove more burdensome to endure than for others. It might prove challenging for you to manage injuries, familial issues, and both professional and personal obligations. It is imperative to possess the capacity to effectively surmount adversity. It is of utmost importance that you maintain a positive outlook in order to effectively harness the potential benefits of adversities, as they possess the capacity to refine and strengthen your character. These scenarios have the potential to assist in discerning and separating individuals who lack purpose and exhibit self-centered behavior within your vicinity. Reiterate to yourself that you have the ability to endure these tribulations and that they are advantageous for your growth, rather than succumbing to a sense of despair.

Tolerate Pain

Suffering will inevitably manifest in various facets throughout your life, encompassing physical anguish stemming from injuries, mental depletion, fractured relationships, and similar hardships. It is imperative to possess the capacity to endure hardship and discomfort in one's life, as this has the potential to propel one towards unprecedented levels of achievement. Adversity and challenges frequently mask the path to your achievements. Develop the capacity to endure discomfort, and it will ultimately enhance the fortitude of your psyche. A resilient mindset will empower you to confront each unfortunate occurrence and challenge that arises in your life.

Eliminate an Adverse Surrounding

Thoroughly observe your surroundings to identify the individuals emanating negative energy. There are numerous individuals in your vicinity who take pleasure in disseminating negative information to you. It is ill-advised to entrust these individuals with dominion over one's thoughts. It is imperative that you take charge of the situation and make a concerted effort to distance yourself from these individuals. Should you possess distressing memories of significance, endeavor to alleviate their burden by relocating to a different environment. Make an effort to distance yourself from individuals who possess knowledge of these matters and may recount these occurrences in your presence. Endeavor to establish a degree of separation from these individuals and forge new social connections.

- Fundamental and Advanced Data Visualization Tools

There is a wide array of software tools that have been devised for the purpose of visualizing data. Furthermore, novel visualization solutions continue to be unveiled on a daily basis. Certain items can be obtained at no cost, while others can be acquired for a fee. The various visualization tools have been purposefully designed and developed to cater to varying levels of specialization. Certain tools are suitable for generating rudimentary visual representations, whereas others excel in facilitating intricate visualizations.

Allow us to engage in a thoughtful analysis of these tools:

Fundamental Data Visualization Tools

Tableau

Tableau constitutes one of the data visualization tools accessible within the marketplace. The platform offers Drag and Drop functionality to its users, enabling them to effortlessly create charts, maps, matrix reports, tabular displays, dashboards, and narratives, even without possessing technical expertise.

Using Tableau, it is possible to establish a link to various data sources such as files, Big Data, and relational databases, enabling the acquisition and processing of data. Additionally, it enables instantaneous collaboration and seamless integration of data, lending it a distinctive quality. It is extensively employed for the purposes of visual data analysis within educational institutions, commercial enterprises, and governmental entities.

Prior to commencing with the use of Tableau, it is necessary to install the software onto your computer. It is highly advisable to acquire the Tableau desktop application by visiting the designated Products section page on the official website of Tableau, which can be found at www.tableau.com. A beneficial aspect of this particular tool is that it offers the convenience of a complimentary trial version, readily available for downloading and installation at no cost.

FusionCharts

This is a software library written in JavaScript that facilitates the visualization of data. It stands among the most esteemed market visualization libraries that require payment. This library offers the capability to generate over 90 distinct chart types, and its seamless integration with diverse platforms and frameworks grants users a high degree of flexibility.

FusionCharts boasts an exceptional attribute that sets it apart as the premier visualization tool. Rather than commencing the creation of your chart de novo, you possess a vast array of pre-existing chart templates at your disposal, whereby you simply need to import your data and customize it to discern the underlying trends and patterns present within your dataset.

Datawrapper

This tool is steadily gaining popularity among media stations that utilize charts for the purpose of presenting statistical data. The tool offers a user-friendly interface, enabling users to effortlessly upload their CSV (comma separated values) data and generate uncomplicated charts. Additionally, utilizing this tool enables users to generate maps that can be seamlessly incorporated into various reports.

Visme

This is an additional tool that can assist you in transforming mundane data into captivating content. It affords you the ability to craft captivating presentations, infographics, and various other forms of engaging content.

The tool offers pre-existing templates that are available for utilization with your data. If the necessity arises for you to establish a bespoke design entirely on your own, you can place your trust in the utilization of content blocks. In addition, there will be a wide array of icons, images, and fonts at your disposal.

Highcharts

This particular product necessitates a valid license in order for its usage, similar to the case with FusionCharts. Nevertheless, there is a trial edition available that allows for personal use at no cost. One does not necessitate specialized training in order to utilize this tool. The reason behind its triumph lies in its ability to support various web browsers, allowing users to create and employ visual presentations across different platforms, a feature that is lacking in many contemporary platforms.

Specialized Tools for Visualizing Data

These tools not only facilitate the creation of more sophisticated visualizations but also enable data analysis. Let us delve into these topics:

Sisense

This constitutes an additional visualization instrument, which encompasses comprehensive analytics functionalities across the entire stack. It is a platform that operates on cloud infrastructure and offers the functionality of drag and drop operations. Additionally, it is capable of managing various data sources and has the ability to process natural language queries.

With the utilization of its drag and drop functionality, individuals can seamlessly generate charts, intricate graphics, and various interactive visualizations. It possesses the capability to consolidate various data sources into a single repository, providing convenient accessibility and enabling instantaneous querying through intuitive dashboards. These dashboards can be shared among different organizations, guaranteeing that even employees with limited technical proficiency can obtain responses to their inquiries.

Qlikview

Tableau's most formidable competitor is this company. It is utilized in more than 100 countries, and its user base has expressed great satisfaction with its extensive selection of features and highly adaptable configuration. This implies that there will be a significant time investment required on your part to attain proficiency with the tool and utilize it to its full capacity.

In addition to its exceptional data visualization capabilities, Qlikview offers its users a repertoire of business intelligence, enterprise reporting, and analytics capabilities, while also delivering a streamlined and uncluttered user interface. It is frequently utilized in conjunction with its counterpart software package known as Qliksense, which excels in facilitating data exploration and discovery. In addition, it enjoys significant community backing and boasts an array of third-party resources catering to its users' integration requirements for their projects.

IBM Watson Analytics

This tool is highly effective for data visualization, distinguishing itself through its exceptional natural language processing capabilities. The platform offers functionalities for managing conversational data proficiently, alongside robust data reporting and the construction of comprehensive dashboards. Nevertheless, this particular tool comes with a substantial price tag, making it suitable exclusively for significant data analytics and visualization endeavors.

Power BI

Microsoft offers the Power BI tool as a complimentary resource for individuals and enterprises, aiming to equip them with a means of effectively analyzing and deriving valuable insights from their data. It serves as an effective tool for non-technical business users to consolidate, visualize, examine, and disseminate their data. It offers a user-friendly interface akin to the one provided by Microsoft Excel, and its compatibility with other Microsoft Office tools enhances its utility. Moreover, its versatility enables users to utilize the tool proficiently right from the outset, obviating the necessity for preliminary instruction.

The tool has been specifically engineered and crafted for utilization by proprietors of small and medium-sized enterprises. Additionally, a Power BI Plus option is available for usage, albeit at a modest monthly subscription cost of under $10.00 per license. The tool is available in various iterations, such as Power BI, a web-based SaaS version

(Software as a Service), Power BI Desktop, a downloadable application for Windows 10, and native mobile apps for Android, Windows, and iOS devices.

Power PI is equipped with a myriad of tools that facilitate its seamless integration with an extensive range of data sources, encompassing various Microsoft offerings, Salesforce, and multiple other vendors. The developers possess the capability to effortlessly modify the graphical representation and default visualizations within the reporting tools, encompassing appearance alterations, as well as importing novel tools into the platform.

Grafana

This is a comprehensive data analytics and visualization solution that provides seamless integration with over 30 data sources, encompassing Elasticsearch, Amazon Web Services (AWS), and Prometheus among others.

Please take note that in terms of integrations, Grafana demonstrates superior performance relative to Kibana. Nevertheless, it is important to consider that each system operates optimally when paired with its corresponding data type. Grafana is renowned for its diverse range of metrics that it offers to its users. As a result of this, Grafana has emerged as the preeminent tool among the diverse range of IoT data visualization tools available.

With the utilization of Grafana, users are able to effectively visualize and amalgamate diverse categories of metric data, resulting in the creation of intricate and dynamic dashboards. Its capacity to offer diverse administrative roles renders it commendable for control and monitoring systems as well.

Alerts and notifications may be generated in accordance with a predetermined set of rules. It possesses a plethora of benefits that are advantageous for expediting data analytics, such as the ability to incorporate annotations, generate custom filters, and append metadata to diverse events displayed on the dashboard.

REFLECTIONS OF POSITIVE CONTEMPLATION

For the narrator, kindly observe a 15-second interval between each sentence, unless otherwise specified. The tone of voice ought to be comforting, yet not excessively lethargic.

This constitutes the initial segment of the program. The purpose of this exercise is to assist you in relinquishing any negative emotions and beliefs you may hold, thereby enabling you to uncover the latent positive aspects that lie beneath them.

Prior to commencing, it is imperative to ascertain a suitable stance wherein you may unwind and remain at ease for the ensuing half-hour.

If possible, kindly proceed to close your eyes or direct your attention towards an object within your immediate surroundings.

It is advised to abstain from attempting to purge one's mind, as this endeavor may yield counterproductive outcomes and generate feelings of discontentment.

Allow yourself to instead acknowledge the thoughts that currently occupy your mind, refraining from any attempts to impede them.

Allow them to approach individually, offer recognition to each of them, and subsequently grant them permission to depart.

In each instance that your thoughts begin to stray during the meditation, kindly ensure to engage in this practice while redirecting your attention towards your breath.

The next step involves breathing in through your nasal passages at a regular rate, followed by a four-second breath retention, and concluding with a gradual exhalation through your oral cavity. (A brief moment of silence, lasting for approximately half a minute.)

Continue practicing this technique until it becomes second nature: breathe in, retain, and exhale slowly. (Speak with a deliberate pace and take a one-minute pause.)

Now, I kindly request that you envision yourself situated within a spacious chamber:

You find yourself in solitude, amidst dim lighting, with the sole perceivable illuminating agent being a solitary candle situated adjacent to a sizeable mirror on the far end of the chamber.

As you progress forward in that particular direction, your proximity to the mirror results in the gradual magnification of your reflection, thereby enlarging its visual presence.

Once you have ultimately traversed the space and positioned yourself directly adjacent to the mirror, allocate a moment to carefully observe and analyze the reflection before you.

May I inquire about the identity of the individual currently situated in your presence? Are you content with the visual aspect of what you are currently observing? Are you content with the reflection that greets you when you gaze into the mirror? Do you harbor deep affection and hold high regard for the individual directly gazing into your eyes? There will be a 20-second hiatus.

I kindly request you to dedicate a brief period of time to engage in a process of deep visualization concerning this alternate version of yourself. Your objective is to establish a strong connection with this envisioned identity, while simultaneously perceiving it from an external perspective. There will be a brief interruption lasting for a duration of twenty seconds.

Please envision the act of bringing one of your hands in contact with the surface of the mirror, while the reflection reciprocates by doing the same from its side, resulting in both palms uniting upon the glass. Once more, take a deep breath in through your nostrils, retain it for a count of four, and then release it slowly through your mouth. (Take a brief intermission for a duration of 30 seconds.)

Allow yourself to experience the profound connection forged by the amalgamation of creative forces, and employ it as a means to establish a long-awaited rapport with your innermost being.

Reflect upon all aspects, whether physical or emotional, that provoke displeasure concerning your present self. Please enumerate any perceived shortcomings concerning your physical attributes and personal characteristics that potentially affect your self-esteem. Additionally, provide a comprehensive explanation of any displeasure you might have towards individuals in your social circle and aspects of your current lifestyle.

Be really specific. Enumerate even the most minor difficulties.

Please allocate an ample amount of time for this task and envision yourself releasing any feelings of frustration, anger, resentment, or disappointment that you may have, directed towards the reflection of your own self in the mirror.

Observe as the mirrored image gradually displays signs of aging and frailty, its physique distorted due to the burden of pervasive negative emotions, its countenance marked by an acrid sense of resentment and disillusionment.

Release any residual pain or sorrow, allowing them to dissipate within the mirror's confines, and cleanse yourself of all lingering negative sentiments while observing the reflection progressively age, its visage swiftly transforming before your very eyes.

Now take a moment to carefully observe the individual standing before you: notice how they have undergone transformations due to the burden of adverse emotions, life encounters, personal evaluations, and external influences.

Observe this individual who is currently burdened by a multitude of negative emotions; sense the bond that exists between you and them.

I now request that you place your hand upon your heart and allow yourself to embrace and be receptive to the visuals before you.

Discover all the affirmative sentiments residing within you - the benevolence, affection, pardon, and comprehension that delineate you more significantly than the entirety of those adverse emotions from which you have recently freed yourself.

Allow this encompassing positive energy to permeate your being; recognize your inherent worthiness and compassion, and allow the accumulation of this positive energy to converge within the grasp of your hand.

Envision yourself channeling this radiant illumination into the mirror, directed towards your image, which presently experiences distress.

Bestow upon it your utmost love and gratitude for its ability to endure your suffering and bear its weight on your behalf.

Extend forgiveness for any transgressions and errors that it may have committed while exerting its utmost efforts, and provide reassurance of your unwavering affection and acceptance.

Provide the utmost of your abilities to alleviate its suffering. Please ensure that you assert your presence to provide solace and comfort, as you possess the most intimate knowledge of your own image and its inherent value.

See your mirrored image start to believe that there is still love in their life, that someone cares and believes in them.

Observe as the facial lines of your reflected likeness fade away; the affection bestowed and reciprocated... the trust and conviction restored.

Observe how the influx of positive energy empowers them to assume a more elevated stance, deriving a sense of deep satisfaction from the inner illumination that is now flourishing within them.

Express your sincere appreciation to the image for its perseverance amidst challenges and adversities, as well as for the valuable lessons it has imparted, resulting in personal growth and increased wisdom.

Observe the illumination returning to your being, as anguish transforms into mindfulness, and sorrow and resentment morph into fortitude and determination.

Allow yourself to be infused with this collective energy, experiencing its powerful flow through your palm as it enters your heart.

Experience the profound emotions of affection and divine favor, as well as the deep connection that presently exists between you and all the facets of your authentic being; cultivate a genuine gratitude for your true essence, both in the present moment and in the future.

Allow the unwavering belief in your abilities and authentic self to envelop you, while you gaze upon the reflection presented in the mirror. Observe the epitome of your being, embodying strength, vitality, love, and a profound appreciation for every aspect of your being.

You may now relinquish that image, expressing your appreciation and assuredness in the conviction that it shall continually be accessible to you, ready to provide aid and serve as a reminder of your true essence whenever needed.

It is with proximity that assistance shall be provided to ensure that you duly acknowledge and value every facet of your being, as each contributes to your authentic self and engenders your distinctiveness within this world.

Please allocate a brief period of time at present to honor and acknowledge your own achievements and allow yourself to experience the abundance of constructive energy permeating your being. (Allow me a moment to collect my thoughts.)

I kindly request that you recollect and internalize the current state of your emotions and cognition, as it shall serve as the initial milestone in our pursuit towards cultivating optimistic thoughts and attaining psychological contentment.

If possible, employ a designated term to elucidate this sentiment, as it will facilitate the prompt return of your subconscious mind to this state whenever desired or necessary. Please employ a succinct and evocative phrase, and rehearse it internally on three occasions.

Direct your attention back to your breathing, inhaling deeply to fill your lungs and then exhaling gradually, thereby relieving any remaining tension.

Subsequently, inhale at your regular rate via the nostrils, retain the breath for a duration of four seconds, and subsequently exhale gradually once more through the oral cavity.

Take a deep breath, retain it, and gradually release it.

Once more, take a deep breath in via your nasal passages, maintain the inhalation for a count of four, and subsequently release the breath slowly through your oral cavity.

Reiterate this sequence several times or until you experience a complete state of relaxation and centeredness once more. There will be a 30-second pause.

Once you have achieved a state of calm and regular breathing, redirect your attention towards your physical presence in the room. Take notice of the sensation of your heartbeat beneath the palm of your hand, the flow of energy coursing through your body, and the restoration of your consciousness to the present moment.

Gently elongate your muscles, starting from the top of your head and moving down to the tips of your toes.

Perform a gentle exercise by moving your limbs in a controlled manner to restore your complete presence in the surrounding environment, attentively perceiving the auditory stimuli and olfactory sensations present in the room.

Allow yourself a brief extension of time, and, upon reaching a state of readiness, proceed to unseal your eyes or redirect your attention away from the selected object of concentration.

Please rise gradually and proceed to firmly stamp your feet upon the floor as a means of reestablishing your connection with the ground.

Cultivate self-love and express gratitude toward yourself, allowing for the experience of love and serenity.

The Scientific Principles Underlying Visualization: Exploring The Mechanisms Of Visualization

The concept of visualization has been extensively discussed for numerous years. The general consensus among individuals is that visualizing success or achieving the desired outcome is conducive to achieving success. For those individuals who criticize visualization as mere speculation and question the rationale behind visualization, we possess scientific evidence that supports our claims. Indeed, there exists a scientific foundation elucidating the rationale and mechanisms through which visualization yields positive effects on individuals.

Visualization can be defined as the overarching concept which encompasses the mental creation of an image without engaging in physical enactment. You are capable of mentally conceptualizing precisely what you desire. Eric Franklin, the individual responsible for establishing the Franklin method, which utilizes the application of imagery and visualization techniques to stimulate both bodily and cognitive functions, asserts that the act of implanting a thought within one's mind and fostering its development will effectively enhance one's overall performance. When an action is visualized, it induces activation in the same cerebral region as when the action is performed physically. For instance, in the process of mental visualization of raising the right hand, the neurological region that becomes stimulated is identical to the region that activates during physical execution of the hand movement. Therefore, the act of envisioning a particular action stimulates neural activity in the brain, akin to actually carrying out the action.

Researchers have devoted extensive time and effort towards the examination and exploration of visualization methodologies. In order to gain a comprehensive understanding of the mechanics of this visualization, it is imperative that we acquire a profound comprehension of the intricate workings of our neural framework. This will provide us with astounding insights into the mechanisms and rationale behind the efficacy of visualization, which is widely regarded as one of the most effective techniques for personal development. The brain is the most intricate organ within the human anatomy. Each study conducted on the functionality of the human brain imparts novel and captivating insights into its true operations. The organ known as the brain consists of cellular structures referred to as neurons. Typically, these neurons exhibit concordance and contribute to the execution of a specific function. When we acquire new knowledge, neuronal connections are formed within our brain, resulting in the establishment of a mapping process. Additionally, when we employ said proficiency, the identical neural circuits are stimulated to facilitate the execution of the assignment.

As we continue to engage in the neural circuit, its strength increases, rendering the recollection process more effortless. This implies that if we are unable to retrieve a skill or information, then we have not acquired it proficiently. Consequently, visualization is effective when implementing this technique. When one repeatedly envisions an idea, the brain begins to react to said idea as though it were tangible. This phenomenon occurs because the thalamus, which functions as the sensory processor within our brain, does not differentiate between actual realities and the perceptions that originate within our cognitive processes. Therefore, when we repeatedly conceptualize an idea, that idea manifests as reality for the brain and consequently elicits corresponding responses. This enhances the feasibility of your concept within your own cognition and instills a sense of motivation to actively pursue its manifestation in the physical realm.

Create a visual representation within your mind. Furthermore, there exists an additional rationale behind the effortless recognition of your concept within your brain when it is repeatedly conveyed - namely, your ability to mentally visualize it. That's right. When one generates a mental representation, they facilitate cognitive processes in two distinct manners. To begin with, given that the human brain does not discriminate between the real experience and the mental imagery, it merely establishes neural pathways to execute the desired action. Secondly, when one envisions something, the typical mode of thought is presented in visual imagery, which is highly advantageous given that the brain tends to comprehend more effectively when presented with visual stimuli. Visualization facilitates the development of neural networks within the cerebral cortex, and these interconnections serve as the foundation, akin to a blueprint, for the execution of real-world behaviors. An additional significant attribute of visualization resides in the incessant repetition of the mental formation, thus bolstering the potency of the resulting imagery.

Additionally, since the neural circuits within your brain have already been formed through the process of visualizing your idea, your idea or thought may appear more familiar. As the level of visualization intensifies, the robustness of the neural connections improves, enabling you to execute your idea in real-time. Visualization, as a cognitive tool, can be effectively utilized across various disciplines to facilitate the process of acquiring knowledge and enhancing comprehension. The process of mentally perceiving or creating mental images significantly influences the cognitive functioning of the brain. Your motor control, attention, perception, and memory have been stimulated. To clarify, the human brain is conditioned to exhibit real-time functionality while engaging in the process of mental visualization.

The neurocognitive associations facilitated by the act of visualization aid in surmounting cognitive barriers, apprehensions, and distress that impede the performance of tasks. It has the potential to enhance your motivation, induce relaxation in your mind and body, enhance your self-assurance, improve self-effectiveness, and optimize motor performance. Essentially, the practice of visualization can serve as a crucial factor in attaining success by fostering a positive mindset conducive to accomplishing one's goals. When the process of visualizing occurs, it leads to the generation of alpha waves in the brain. These waves aid in inducing a state of relaxation and enhancing one's focus. Alpha waves are additionally accountable for alleviating anxiety and stress. They can additionally diminish discomfort and enhance enjoyment. The process of visualization instills fresh memories within your brain, encompassing images that have the potential to be advantageous for your mental state. By engaging in the process of mental imagery to depict triumph, attaining a desired objective, or executing a given assignment with efficacy, your cerebral cortex forges neural associations that cultivate a belief in your accomplishment. This practice is recognized to boost one's self-assurance and foster a greater sense of certainty in carrying out the aforementioned task. Through iterated visualizations of a progression of images that depict your intended outcome, you develop a genuine conviction in the attainability and reality of these images. Additionally, the process of visualization obstructs extraneous neural and sensory information that does not pertain to the intended idea or objective. This implies that inconsequential thoughts and anxieties are filtered, thus facilitating a heightened level of concentration on the objective. It additionally heightens your inherent drive to accomplish it, thereby diminishing the perception of the goal as unattainable. Concentration is a primary advantage of visualization, as the act of visualization necessitates the directed focus on a single object or idea. They have the capability to stimulate cognitive activity in comprehending the circumstances, facilitating your alignment with a state of non-judgmental awareness.

Ultimately, the process of visualization allows the mind to perceive the scenario as though it were manifesting in reality. Therefore, the neural activity in your brain stimulates the regions associated with feelings of happiness, increased productivity, and enhanced self-confidence. Essentially, your cognitive processes primarily rely on visual representations. When one narrates a tale spanning a thousand words, it becomes impracticable to encompass every single detail, but rather prompts the formation of vivid mental imagery and captivates the cognitive faculties until the conclusion. Moreover, the faculties of your mind lack the capacity to discern between the genuine experience of something and the mere act of imagining it. This is the reason why visualization proves to be highly effective for us.

HOW VISUALIZATION WORKS?

Envision a scenario where certain dreams that occur during the period of sleep are actualized. Possibly, you engaged in a conversation with an acquaintance within a dream, wherein the details were indistinct, yet the setting was evident. Suppose, for the sake of argument, that said conversation had indeed taken place in a realm apart from the present context. Suppose your companion subsequently informed you that they had conversed with you within a dream, and upon further reflection, you discovered that your dream experiences were indeed congruent.

If specific locations or motifs consistently manifest in your dreams, what do you believe they are conveying to you? You possess exceptional interpretive abilities when it comes to your own dreams. I frequently experience a recurring dream wherein I am traversing the city on a bicycle, inadvertently neglecting to bring along a security device for it. I reach destinations where I must securely bring my bicycle indoors to prevent theft. My understanding is that I am being cautioned about exposing myself and being susceptible. The dream occasionally resurfaces. Occasionally, there may be a considerable passage of time between occurrences of these dreams, yet they resurface when they bear relevance to specific events unfolding at present.

While positive affirmations facilitate the formulation of new beliefs, visualization enables the mental construction of one's actualized existence within these beliefs. Subsequently, your cognitive faculties encode these mental images as genuine and credible. You have the ability to observe yourself speaking and acting with confidence. One can observe oneself becoming a more resilient individual in their daily existence.

The human brain is anatomically and functionally compartmentalized into two distinct hemispheres: the left hemisphere, associated with logical thinking, and the right hemisphere, associated with creative processes. The majority of our existence is dedicated to utilizing the left hemisphere, engaging in the logical and rational resolution of challenges and the accomplishment of duties, employing verbal expression and conceptual understanding. The right hemisphere perceives the world through visual stimuli and is connected with emotional responses. Visualization employs visuals and emotions as a means of acquiring preparation for real-life execution.

Visualization entails the perception of vibrant, multicolored, and vivid imagery depicting one's desired state. Your mind perceives these mental images as authentic and credible. Given that the human mind aligns its internal and external images to maintain consistency, it will endeavor to align your external reality with your newly-formed mental reality.

Strategies for Enhancing the Effectiveness of Visualization

Believe in yourself

If one comprehends that the human body is incessantly influenced by the power of the mind, and that the brain cannot distinguish between what is real and what is imagined, it becomes apparent that the mind is not a vague and intangible entity that merely interprets life events, but rather a force that actively instigates alterations in the physical body. By adopting this approach, you cultivate a sense of confidence in your own abilities, wherein your thoughts, aspirations, and intentions bear tangible outcomes.

One can only execute the task correctly.

A considerable number of individuals hold the belief that they lack the ability to visualize due to the assumption that everyone else perceives their surroundings in high definition (HD). Trust me, they don't. However, it is the action carried out by them that leads us to believe that our approach might be incorrect. In reality, the majority of individuals merely acquire an ambiguous collection of visuals. The foremost consideration lies in your intention and ensuring that you do not harbor any doubts regarding your proficiency in the matter. I prefer the term 'imagine' over 'visualize' due to the fact that each individual engages in imagination uniquely.

Relax

This could be more challenging than initially suggested, however, implementing a consistent regimen of relaxation greatly contributes to mitigating stress in the body, thereby yielding favorable outcomes. Meditation and yoga are highly commendable practices. Engaging in physical activity can also serve as an effective means of relaxation. Maintaining a well-balanced and nutritious diet can be beneficial, characterized by the absence of stimulants and excessive amounts of sugar and saturated fat.

Lighten up

I frequently propose that individuals incorporate a small measure of levity into their visualizations. This alleviates concerns regarding potential malfunction. When we experience apprehension, we stimulate cerebral regions linked to feelings of fear and anxiety. If we incorporate a modicum of lightheartedness into the process of visualization, we maintain our focus on the envisioned scenario and, potentially, facilitate the redirection of our brain networks away from anxiety centers. This, in turn, may engender a sense of optimism and hope instead of worry. I strongly urge individuals to engage in the act of performing a 'triumphal dance' with the aim of bringing their visualization to a conclusion. Essentially, upon completion, it is customary to perform a lighthearted celebratory dance and continue doing so until a smile graces your countenance. This facilitates the stimulation of a sense of brightness within the brain.

The three Rs - Iteration-Iteration-Iteration

Studies indicate that repetitive mental visualization of movements has the ability to modify the structure of the brain. Neuroimaging data of individuals actively engaging in piano playing compared to individuals mentally simulating piano playing revealed comparable alterations occurring within identical cerebral regions. However, in order to achieve the necessary modifications, it is essential to consistently repeat the physical or mental actions involved. When the cessation of work occurs, the cerebral regions undergo a subsequent reduction in size. Consistency is crucial in this regard. One does not attain the status of an Olympic champion through a single visit to the gym. Engaging in consistent visualization practice is crucial to achieve optimal outcomes.

The Cognizant And Unconscious Mind

Based on multiple research studies, it has been observed that the mind operates on three distinct levels. The study was conducted in a theoretical manner, given the inherent challenges in explaining the intricate workings of the human mind. The examination of human consciousness can be effectively conducted by employing the analogy of the triangle.

The vertices of the triangle are analogous to our conscious mind, which occupies a relatively limited region within the space. It pertains to the notion that only 10 percent of our brain's functioning is attributable to our conscious mind. There exists a limited area beneath our conscious mind, often denoted as the preconscious mind.

The preconscious or subconscious mind governs approximately 50 to 60 percent of our cognitive processes within the brain. Beneath this level of the preconscious mind, lies a region known as the unconscious. Therefore, the subconscious mind is responsible for approximately 30-40% of cerebral activity. This particular region of the brain exhibits considerable depth and obscurity, rendering it the least susceptible to conscious cognitions.

The conscious mind is commonly regarded as the controller or overseer of the brain.

By means of this region of the brain, individuals are capable of comprehending and establishing connections with others. This particular region of the brain assumes the role of interfacing with the external environment via the use of visuals, empirical information, numerical data, written and verbal expressions, cognitive processes, and motor actions.

In contrast, the subconscious mind is postulated to function as a repository within the brain.

It meticulously records and retains all recollections and prior occurrences associated with a particular traumatic event or ordinary incident, which have been unintentionally disregarded by the conscious realm of the brain and are presently deemed insignificant to the individual. The subliminal or the preconscious components of the cerebral organ maintain constant interaction with the unconscious component of the cerebral organ.

An individual's beliefs, attitudes, habits, and behaviors are shaped by the recollections and encounters residing within the realm of the preconscious mind. The unconscious mind establishes communication with the conscious mind by means of the subconscious mind. This interaction is the cornerstone of imbuing meaning into people's engagement with the surrounding world.

It allows individuals to establish interpersonal connections and engage with their surroundings and fellow beings by means of emotions, sentiments, sensory experiences, creative insights, and aspirations.

Below, an in-depth elucidation of each of the three tiers of consciousness has been provided:

The concept of the conscious mind remains undefined as of yet, as no definitive definition has been established thus far. Nevertheless, it has been suggested that the distinguishing factor between the conscious mind and the preconscious or unconscious mind lies in the state of being "aware."

However, it would be incorrect to label the subconscious mind as lacking awareness. Numerous studies have been conducted which illustrate the impact of the environment and surroundings on individuals, even during the administration of anesthesia or in a state of deep slumber. There are instances where an individual arrives at their destination through driving, yet acquires no recollection of the journey upon arrival.

In such instances, it is the realm of the subconscious mind that assumes awareness and assumes responsibility for executing all requisite functions. It is widely acknowledged that the conscious mind is responsible for the faculties of logical reasoning and cognitive processing. Despite this observation, there remains no discernible distinction between the conscious, subconscious, and unconscious mind.

The unconscious mind is further regarded as the repository of all emotions, memories, and habits, thereby endowing it with the capacity for the execution of rational inference and cogent thought processes. Let us acquire comprehension of the functioning of the conscious mind by means of an illustrative instance - During the initial stages of human life, when individuals are in infancy, the developmental progress of the conscious section of the brain is incomplete, rendering it inadequate for the evaluation and assessment of the entirety of environmental information.

In this phase, it is primarily the unconscious and subconscious aspects of the mind that carry out the majority of functions, such as recognizing the nipple or bottle as a source of nourishment, comprehending that crying elicits attention from caregivers, interpreting parental cuddling as an expression of security and affection, and various other abilities.

Therefore, in this stage, it is the unconscious and subconscious faculties that exert considerable effort, facilitating the development of crucial logical patterns of association that are integral to their future survival. Based on extensive research and scholarly discourse, it has been ascertained that the subconscious mind plays a pivotal role in executing two primary functions that are unique to this particular facet of the psyche.

The following information is outlined below:

1. Diverting Your Attention: It is widely acknowledged that the subconscious mind exhibits greater activity in evoking an awareness of the surroundings in comparison to the conscious mind and

possesses the capacity to function even during states of sleep. Nevertheless, it is crucial to have knowledge and comprehension of the reality that the subconscious mind operates under the directives of the conscious mind. For example, in the event that your conscious thoughts exhibit negativity, it follows that your subconscious mind will also impart emotions, sentiments, and thoughts that align with this negative thinking pattern. By means of this process, the sentiment and passion shall manifest tangibly, and should an individual's mental faculties prove insufficient in surmounting adversities, they may find themselves entrapped within an interminable cycle of pessimism, unease, and trepidation.

There exist individuals who possess the capability to sustain a favorable emotional state and perceive the circumstances in their lives as favorable. An individual's perception of their life is greatly influenced by the programming of their subconscious and unconscious mind during infancy. The capacity of the conscious mind to actively determine its emotional states, such as whether it experiences positivity or negativity, happiness or anger, or embraces pessimism or optimism, stands out as a preeminent and potent faculty of the human mind. The ideas that an individual formulates and retains in their consciousness are regarded as one of the inherent liberties inherent to the human condition. An individual who finds themselves incarcerated in an environment marked by deteriorating and cruel circumstances possesses the capacity to attain mental liberation by consciously redirecting their thoughts.

The Significance of Creative Visualization: An Exploration of Its Origins and the Importance of Incorporating it Into Your Daily Routine

What is creative visualization? Diverse individuals hold varying interpretations of creative visualization as both a concept and an application. However, the concept of creative visualization entails harnessing the cognitive capacity of the mind and eliciting its imaginative capabilities to manifest aspirations and objectives into reality.

In the practice of creative visualization, one harnesses the faculties of the subconscious mind to conceive or construct diverse scenarios internally. Utilizing one's aptitude for visualization entails the process of constructing a vivid mental representation of a concept or object, subsequently concentrating one's attention upon this visualization for a designated period. What this accomplishes is it exerts beneficial impacts on an individual's cognition and perspective. This actually enables individuals to bring about changes in the external world through the practice of creative visualization.

Through the practice of creative visualization, it is conceivable to alter the pattern of energy and effectively channel it towards the achievement of one's objectives and aspirations at a significantly accelerated pace, exceeding previous expectations.

Were you aware that a significant majority, approximately 80%, of affluent and influential individuals encompassing a global scale have employed the technique of creative visualization at some point during their personal growth and achievement of their life objectives? I am confident that this has piqued your interest, and you are eager to comprehend the mechanics behind it.

The mechanics of this process are more straightforward than one might assume. Are you aware of the fact that the subconscious mind readily embraces the pre-existing contents of the conscious mind? It does. In fact, a more precise elucidation would be as follows: upon earnestly embracing a particular thought, it inherently holds the capacity to engender a transformation in both one's cognitive disposition and the behavioral patterns exhibited by one's physical being.

Consequently, you find yourself establishing connections with diverse individuals and encountering a variety of situations and circumstances. The power of thoughts possesses the capacity to architect one's life in accordance with the nature of one's thoughts.

One's thoughts transition or migrate from the conscious realm to the subconscious realm. Consequently, it is feasible for any optimistic thoughts one envisions to subliminally transmit from oneself to an individual who may possess the capability to support the achievement of one's objectives, aspirations, and wishes. This aligns with the understanding that you are an integral component of the divine force responsible for the creation of the cosmos.

Despite the seemingly fantastical nature of this concept, its underlying principles are inherently straightforward. Please take a moment to embrace the concept that you are a vital component of the vast cosmic force. This implies that the nature of the universe is influenced by thoughts, thus suggesting that the manifestation of one's thoughts is a reality. Does this imply that all of your thoughts manifest into reality? Negative. Only thoughts that possess clear and precise definition, concentration, and repetition manifest into reality.

This unequivocally demonstrates that thoughts can be understood as forms of energy. More so, focused thoughts. This implies that a positive thought infused with emotional energy possesses the capability to alter the equilibrium of surrounding energy. This can subsequently result in alterations to our surroundings or circumstances, contingent upon our intended realization.

It is important to observe that numerous individuals have a tendency to reiterate specific thoughts on a daily basis, and the content of our thoughts frequently contributes to altering the surrounding environment and circumstances. By harnessing the power of creative visualization, individuals have the ability to generate and reconfigure various scenarios, circumstances, and events.

Although this might appear unduly intricate, it is, in fact, quite straightforward. Consider viewing it in the context of repeatedly watching a cinematic production. Through repeated viewings of a film, one can discern scenes or particulars that may have eluded initial detection, and alternatively, one can envision various scenarios or alternate realities.

It should be duly emphasized that one can effectively alter their reality by manipulating their mental imagery and thought processes. Indeed, every individual possesses the capability to modify or manipulate their own perception of the world.

Does this imply, by any chance, that creative visualization is akin to mystical or supernatural practices? The truth is no. You are not employing supernatural or mystical abilities.

What you are effectively engaging in is harnessing the vast potential of inherent abilities possessed by all individuals, albeit largely left untapped. Does this imply the ability to alter every aspect? Regrettably, it is not permissible to modify an object of tangible nature. You have the ability to enact transformative change and reconfigure your surroundings.

For instance, if you reside in a compact dwelling and require a more spacious residence. Rather than complaining and being preoccupied with concerns about your destiny and financial constraints, it is imperative that you alter your mindset and perspective. Begin by envisioning yourself residing in a spacious apartment. This is very easy. So effortless that it resembles idle daydreaming.

Taking this comprehension into account, let us examine the historical background of this innovative visualization technique.